The Thinking TREE

www.DyslexiaGames.com

Dyslexia Games Series B-Book 5
Friendly Copyright Notice:

The Thinking Tree LLC   ●   617 N Swope St.   ●   Greenfield, IN 46140   ●   info@dyslexiagames.com   ●   +1 (317) 622-8852

Art & Animals

Learn to draw animals while developing the important skills necessary for reading and writing success.

By Sarah J. Brown

Parent Teacher Instructions:

Provide the student with a set of sharp colored pencils, sharp pencil, and a fine point black pen. Some of the details are very small, so having a fine point pen or pencil is very important.

Read the instructions on the first four pages to the student. After introducing the child to the first few lessons he should be able to complete the lessons on his own. Talk to the child about his favorite animals as well as yours. Ask him questions about the animals he likes best.

These exercises develop tracking skills, thinking skills, and writing skills. The lessons also introduce cursive writing and include several number games. The games also work to teach the child to be precise and perceptive while paying attention to details.

Children learn to write letters, words and numbers while tapping into the creative area of their minds.

Use colored pencils to add color to the animal that you like best:

Frog

Guinea Pig

Complete the pattern:

Name: _____ **Date:** _____

What's Missing? Complete the Drawing:

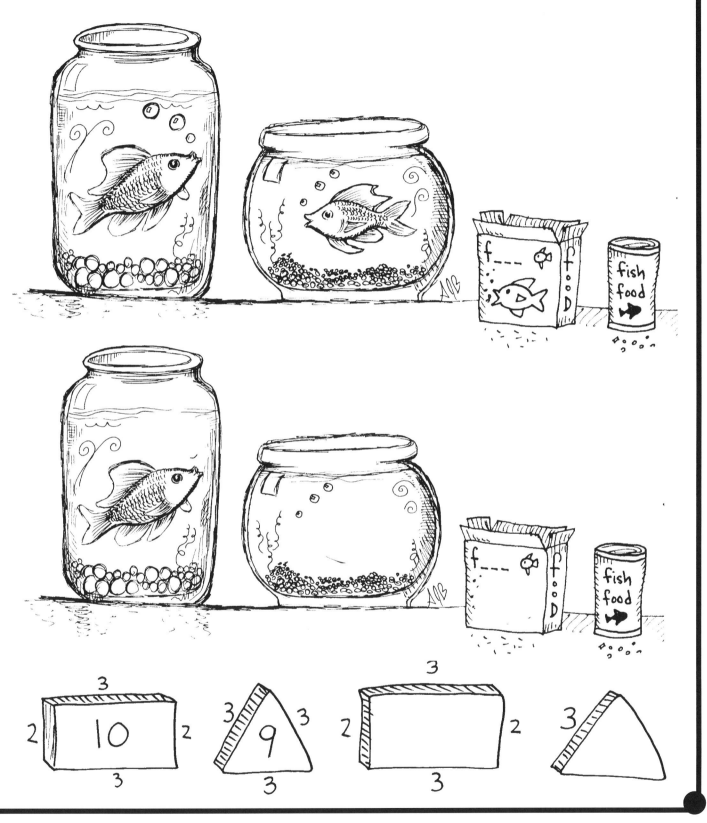

Name:_____ Date:_____

Use colored pencils to add color to the animal that you like best:

Puppy

Goat

Complete the pattern:

Name:_____ Date:_____

What's Missing? Complete the Drawing:

Name: _____ Date: _____

Use colored pencils to add color to the animal that you like best:

Dolphin

Duck

Complete the pattern:

Name:_____   Date:_____

What's Missing? Complete the Drawing:

Name:_____   Date:_____

What's Missing? Complete the Drawing:

Name:_____ **Date:_____**

What's Missing? Complete the Drawing:

dog food

d_g f__d

doggie treat

Name:_____ **Date:**_____

Use colored pencils to add color to the animal that you like best:

Hamster

Rabbit

Complete the pattern:

Name:_____   Date:_____

Use colored pencils to add color to the animal that you like best:

Blue Jay

Turtle

Complete the patterns:

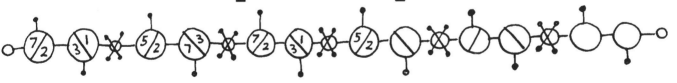

Name:_____ Date:_____

What's Missing? Complete the Drawing:

Name:_____ **Date:**_____

Use colored pencils to add color to the animal that you like best:

Rabbit

Frog

Complete the pattern:

Name:_____ Date:_____

What's Missing? Complete the Drawing:

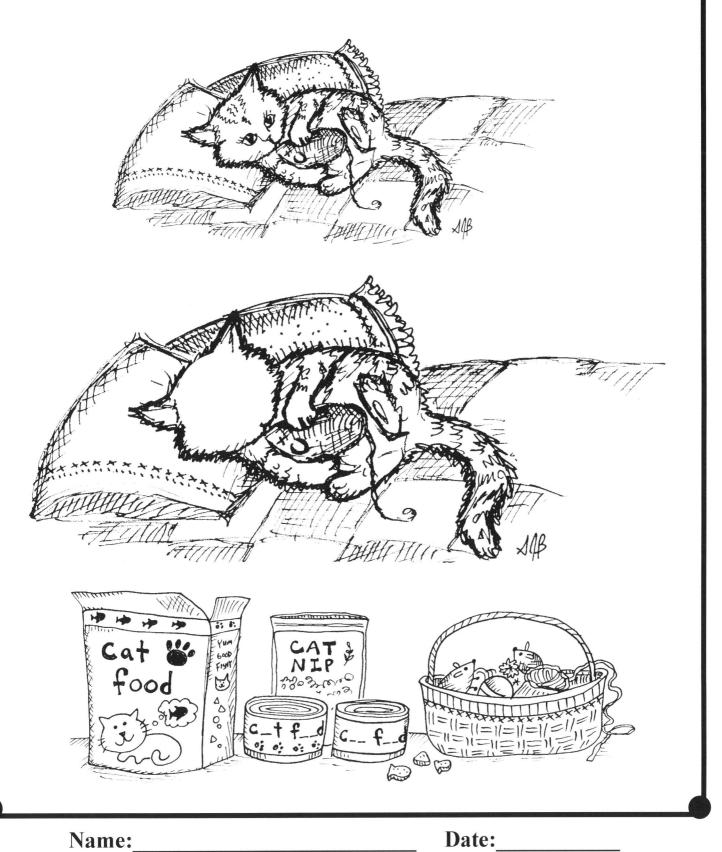

Name:_____ Date:_____

Use colored pencils to add color to the animal that you like best:

Mouse

Lamb

Complete the pattern:

Name:_____ **Date:**_____

What's Missing? Complete the Drawing:

Name:_____ **Date:**_____

What's Missing? Complete the Drawing:

Horse

horse

Puppy

Horse

horse

Puppy

Name: _____ **Date:** _____

Use colored pencils to add color to the animal that you like best:

Kitten

Rooster

Complete the pattern:

Name:_____   Date:_____

What's Missing? Complete the Drawing:

Name:_____ Date:_____

Use colored pencils to add color to the animal that you like best:

Pig

Squirrel

Complete the pattern:

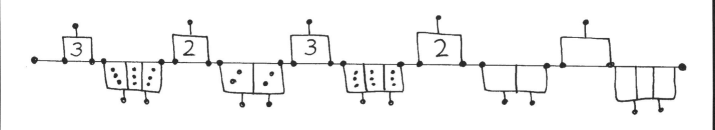

Name:_____ **Date:**_____

What's Missing? Complete the Drawing:

Name:_____ **Date:**_____

Use colored pencils to add color to the animal that you like best:

Snail

Horse

Complete the pattern:

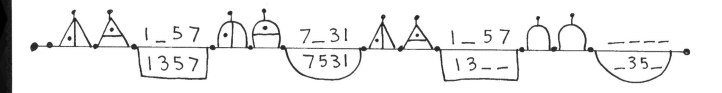

1_57   7_31   1_57
1357   7531   13__   _35_

Name:_____   Date:_____

What's Missing? Complete the Drawing:

Name:_____ Date:_____

Use colored pencils to add color to the animal that you like best:

Butterfly

Toad

Complete the pattern:

Name:_____ **Date:**_____

What's Missing? Complete the Drawing:

Name:_____ **Date:**_____

Use colored pencils to add color to the animal that you like best:

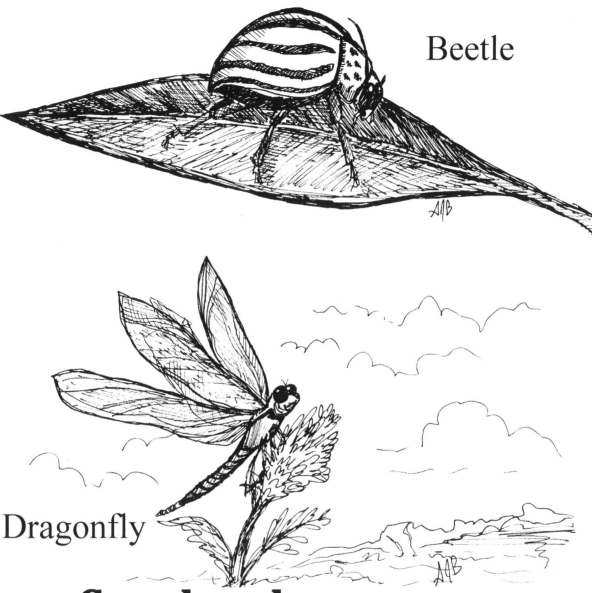

Beetle

Dragonfly

Complete the pattern:

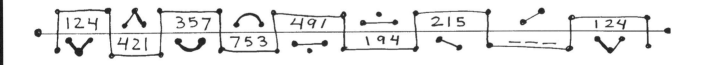

Name:_____ Date:_____

What's Missing? Complete the Drawing:

Write the Missing Words:

1. tree
1.

2. house
2.

3. fence
3.

4. hills
4.

5. lamb
5.

6. rabbits
6.

7. swing
7.

8. cloud
8.

9. road
9.

10. flowers
10.

Name:_____ Date:_____

Use colored pencils to add color to the animal that you like best:

Robin

Sheep

Complete the pattern:

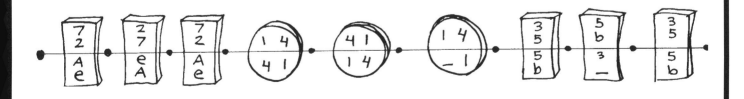

Name:_____ **Date:**_____

What's Missing? Complete the Drawing:

Write the Missing Words:

house	swing	Rabbits	Hills
house	swing	rabbits	hills
h_ _ _ _ _	_ _ _ _ _	_ _ _ _ _	_ _ _ _

Name:_____ **Date:**_____

Use colored pencils to add color to the animal that you like best:

Dog

Bunny

Complete the pattern:

Name:_____ Date:_____

Use colored pencils to add color to the animal that you like best:

Butterfly

Pony

Complete the pattern:

Name:_____ **Date:**_____

Art & Animals

Creative Games
For Thinkers, Artists & Animal Lovers

Certificate of Completion

_____

Name & Age

_____

Date of Completion

The Thinking
TREE

_____

Dyslexia Games

_____

Teacher

The Thinking
TREE

www.DyslexiaGames.com

Created by: Sarah Janisse Brown

Made in the USA
Columbia, SC
24 May 2025